The Angel Asked God

The Angel Asked God

Vera Littlewood

Writer's Showcase
San Jose New York Lincoln Shanghai

The Angel Asked God

Writer's Showcase
an imprint of iUniverse.com, Inc.

For information address:
iUniverse.com, Inc.
5220 S 16th, Ste. 200
Lincoln, NE 68512
www.iuniverse.com

ISBN: 0-595-19246-7

Printed in the United States of America

Contents

Preface

At some point in our lives we all ask the question, "Who are you God?" and "Where are you?"

These questions are becoming more evident as the future holds a greater amount of uncertainty for more and more people. Questions have also arisen as to upcoming anticipated events. Issues that deal with earth changes or social changes.

In any case, each individual is finding it clear that a personal satisfaction must be found in obtaining answers for a fulfilling and rewarding life.

The following pages present a poetic story of an angel that asked the very same questions and the answers that were given. The entire message is based on the concept of love and the simple spirit of co-operation.

This book is a paean for the reader. It is sure to bring happiness and delight to all those that read and reread.

Acknowledgements

I would like to dearly thank the following people for their support and kindness:

Peter Boseley

Pat Gleeson

Arthur Eakin

Reverend Gloria Brough

Reverend Martin Brough

Dr. Neil Tessler

My family

Introduction

I was inspired to write this book.

I have had years of spiritual and religious background, it is life that has been my greatest teacher.

Through all the hardships and suffering that I encountered, I gained a greater understanding of what faith, hope and love mean.

I have had experience in business, science and the arts. But the greatest career has been a mother to three lovely children. Life taught me the importance of valuing every friendship and treating every encounter with a smile.

I hope that you as a reader will gain more understanding and never give up hope, faith and above all, love in your life.

V. Littlewood

When faced
with

a challenge.

We are forced to

face

the mirror.

V. Littlewood

The Angel Asked God

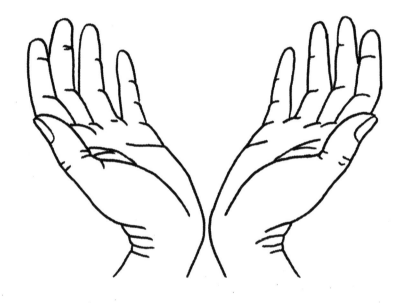

Chapter 1

The Angel Asked God

In the night, a lonely angel walked slowly

through a dimly candle lit room,

to a mirror beside an open window.

The angel looked into the mirror but saw no wings.

Dismayed, the angel asked God,

"Dear God, why can't you just pick up this whole earth

into your loving hands, and stop all the hardship?

And just forgive everyone?"

No response was heard.

In great sadness the angel knelt down and said,

"This morning I felt the greatest sense of loss,

as I realized that I was without hope.

None of my dreams have been fulfilled."

"This morning I felt so weary,

as I realized that I was without faith.

I've lived through more hardship than I ever expected."

"This morning I ached in loneliness,

as I realized my love never came.

Many times I've prayed for love and found none."

"Dear God, are you a distant star?

Where are you?"

The Angel Asked God

Suddenly the winds came howling through the window

blowing the angel's garments into disarray.

The earth began to shake, rattling the mirror.

A crack of thunder was heard and a lightning bolt flashed,

bending it's way into the room.

Then as suddenly as the heavens shook, it all stopped.

A moment of peace resided.

Then a voice answered,

"No. God is much greater than this.

Inside the infinity of an atom—

in the minutest space of an atom—

God is there.

There is a vast world around us

and we must surely abide by the laws of the earth,

the universe, ourselves and foremost

by God's wishes and commands.

God is all powerful, for He is omnipotent.

God is all present, for He is omnipresent.

All needs are taken care of by God.

God does provide everything.

Has God not taken care of everything in the past?

So He shall in the future.

For all things come from God and are for the very best.

God listens and He answers."

Chapter 2

The angel quietly thought for a moment.

Then with a deep sigh, stood up and wearily walked

to a bronzed chair in the middle of the room.

Beside the ornately decorated chair sat a golden harp.

The angel sat down and began to strum a perfect melody.

The notes were soft and sweet to hear.

Then carefully, the angel strummed harder

and the notes became louder.

Then with determination the song was played even harder.

Suddenly one of the strings snapped.

The angel sat back in the chair, looked up and asked,

"Dear God, if you're listening,

then why don't you answer my questions?"

Slowly the earth began to tremble.

The harp began to shake.

More strings snapped as every object in the room vibrated.

The candlelight flickered.

Suddenly the trembling stopped.

The voice answered,

"God answers all those who seek knowledge,

wisdom, grace and understanding.

Be grateful and you shall receive.

People may dream a wish and it will come true,

if they faithfully believe it to be true.

Learn patience, virtue and trust in God.

Trust, seek and you shall find your answers.

God is the only answer in all matters.

He has a hand in all things.

God wishes us to seek understanding.

The Angel Asked God

God is everlasting.

There is nothing else that is.

All the externals around us, even the people around us,

can change at any given moment.

They are all responsibilities that we take on.

When everything around us disappears,

we are always left with the same thing:

ourselves and God.

God knows and understands all.

No truth is undiscovered.

All lies but uncovered.

God is truth and truth is eternal.

He is also love and love is eternal.

God is within us.

God resides in all people's hearts.

His light shines in all of us.

All people belong to God and are made up of God.

Don't force anything.

Let life be a deep let go and life will be richer

and filled with surprises that await you.

Today is but a bunch of memories.

Yesterday is far gone and tomorrow is a bright new future.

Life is like a river running fast

and then slowing down around a bend.

Then look around a corner and see a whole new world!

Life can be exciting and should be for everybody.

It is a journey that God has created for each one of us.

Remember to stop and listen at all times.

God is listening and hears you.

There are no worries with God

as He protects, helps and guides you."

Vera Littlewood

Chapter 3

The angel sighed once more and stood up.

Looking down at the disarrayed robe,

the angel carefully wrapped the sash

back in its place for a more comfortable fit.

Then the angel strode to a globe in the corner of the room.

A beautifully painted earth was on top of a brass stand.

The Angel Asked God

The angel caressed the mountains and the oceans.

Then with a finger, nudged the earth into a spin.

The globe spun effortlessly on its axis.

With another nudge of the hand,

the earth whirled faster.

It spun so quickly it fell off its stand with a crash.

The angel picked up a piece of the globe

and holding it out with both hands, asked,

"Dear God, if there are no worries, then why don't you help

and stop the hardship that surrounds us?"

The wind blew in from outside.

It tossed the angel's hair back and forth.

The candles flickered and blew out.

Then the wind stopped and the distant morning sun

began to shed a glimmer of light.

The voice answered,

"God has a divine purpose and you are in it.

He has a purpose in all things.

Many of his people suffer for a reason.

Truth, honesty and justice do prevail.

Trust in God's understanding and you'll be much happier.

The sooner that you realize that all is well,

the sooner you'll be happy.

God will take care of all things.

Believe and trust in His guidance,

and He will guide you.

You can be sure of that.

Today, tomorrow and forever.

All in all nothing is perfect

and there is a reason for everything

even when we don't see it.

Remember that the sky is always blue

and the heavens are forever –

even when the clouds shadow the sun.

We are here to learn and grow

and we are taught by all people and all situations.

The Angel Asked God

Everything in the galaxy and universe

must have its proper place and time of event.

All things must end and a new beginning formed.

God loves everyone and knows what is in people's hearts.

No creature in God's universe is forgotten.

Great or small is important and all is connected.

Vera Littlewood

All things belong to God.

There is no reason to fret in the world.

All things are taken care of and are granted.

Hand over all things to God—

things work out better that way.

God treats everyone with care and concern.

No one is ever left out. No one.

This is one thing that people forget every time.

Life not only evolves about one concern or thing,

but around many.

That is why it is so important to stay at peace at all times.

Because who knows what might be in store for you next, right?

Make the best choices and go enjoy yourself.

You deserve it!"

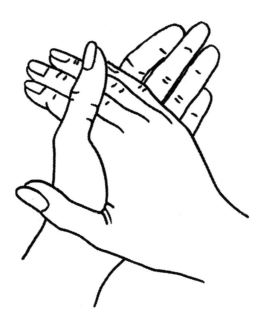

Chapter 4

The angel put down the globe

and stood in solitude for a moment.

After deep consideration,

the angel walked across the room to a waterfall.

A beautifully created stream of water fell down

four tiers of granite rocks, amidst earthen planters.

On the left, stone steps led up to the top of the waterfall

and on the right, were rocks that formed a path to the summit.

The angel looked at both paths and asked,

"Dear God, do I have free will to make my own choices?"

A gust of wind blew across the waterfall

and sprayed a gentle mist of water.

Shimmering droplets fell upon the angel's attire.

Then another gust of wind blew in

and the droplets disappeared.

The voice answered,

"All people are given free will.

It is up to each person to make the right and proper choices

no matter how small they may seem at the time.

Take all things into consideration.

All things come from God

and are for the worldly good of humankind.

God works for the betterment and love of all people.

Treat everything as one—a wholeness—

and all things shall work together for the good.

People can unite for a common cause, if they wish.

Make the best out of now and be grateful.

Keep on living.

Let God lead you in the path you are to go.

It is wiser to follow God's footsteps than your own, always.

For God shall lead you down the middle road—

the golden path—

and He shall guide you in ways unimaginable.

God can work great miracles by the touch of His hand.

All things are possible by the hands of God.

God has no fear, only people do.

That is why it is not possible for people to achieve great things,

only little things by human hands.

God asks people to render themselves true, bold, shining and bright.

So put on a happy face and smile."

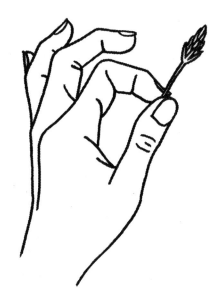

Chapter 5

The Angel Asked God

The angel climbed up the stone steps

alongside the cascading water to the top.

A gentle stream emerged between slabs of slate and granite.

Several more partly constructed stone steps reached higher

into an empty space near the vaulted ceiling.

Many earthen planters sat beside the waterfall,

but only barren earth filled them.

The angel looked at all the barren soil

and then looked up and asked,

"Dear God, you say that I should be happy,

but when I see empty dreams, how can I?"

The ground began to tremble and the waters poured out faster.

Quickly the water jumped from its cascading fall.

More and more water flowed, pushing the stones away.

Then before the water eroded all, it stopped.

The voice answered,

"Learn to smile under all circumstances.

All challenges should be met with a smile on your face.

People need their hearts gladdened.

So smile.

God always knows what is going on.

The Angel Asked God

Look toward tomorrow because the future is already here now.

Tomorrow is a bright, bold and beautiful new day.

Expect the unexpected.

Go forth and enjoy.

Vera Littlewood

Life is supposed to be full of joy and laughter.

Just relax and enjoy.

The miracles work faster and better that way.

Take all things in stride and joy.

Be swift in thought and joyous in heart.

The Angel Asked God

No matter what your present situation is,

you're supposed to be having fun and stopping to smell the roses.

Don't take things too seriously or yourself too seriously.

Don't fret and get engulfed in worries.

Vera Littlewood

If all else fails—pray from the heart—

and your prayer will be answered.

Make yourself more comfortable in the immediate situation.

Always seek out the good in everything that you do.

This life is but a learning experience

and such as this we must all do our very best

with efficiency, love and understanding.

Better yet, lead our lives with God.

Within God, within us, lies all our needs.

All our answers are found within us.

Follow your heart and dreams do come true."

Chapter 6

The angel looked at the winding peaceful waterfall.

Then walked back down the steps to the bottom.

Turning around, the angel looked back at the crystal waters

flowing down beside the planters, empty of flowers.

The angel dug in the dirt with both hands.

Small seeds were in the planters, but none had sprouted.

In earnest thought, the angel asked,

"Dear God, you say that my dreams can come true,

but am I capable?"

The candlelight began to flicker.

A whistling wind danced around the earthen planters.

Dirt was whisked in the air and brushed against the angel's robe.

Then quietly the wind subsided.

The voice answered,

"Success is simply a journey—

a journey of one's spirit, mind, soul

and all of what one gathers along the way.

It matters not how you get there.

But what matters is what you take there.

Never take too much—only what you need and can use.

It is so important to always think positive.

As soon as you allow a negative thought

or fear to enter into your mind,

then you allow a piece of your dream or existence to break away.

If you lose time in doubt, you never gain it back.

Why waste time on negative emotions such as anger or fear?

These are insecurities and rob us of valuable time

that we can never recover.

Time is of the essence,

so don't delay in thinking positive happy thoughts.

Keep faith, God will help you.

All wishes are accepted and dreams come true.

It is only you that need think clearly upon things

and leave all matters in God's hands.

Most people don't know how brave they really are.

All negative emotions such as fear, hurt, sadness and anger

are all due to a lack of understanding.

We do not understand the universe and ourselves enough.

We may not understand each other

but we all have the ability to learn.

In everyone's heart lies an open miracle waiting to be discovered.

Always rely on yourself first and remember that God is with you.

Trust in God.

He will guide you.

Trust your instincts.

They will guide you.

Above all, believe in yourself and in God.

In God, all things are made possible.

Your strength lies in God and in yourself.

You alone can decide your destiny.

Remember, nothing ventured is nothing gained.

The hard part is following through.

Learn discipline.

Keep your head clear and your mind focused.

Things will come to you as you need them.

Keep control of your emotions

and be ready to meet all challenges.

When examining emotions, one can ask,

what is the best way to handle this?

Remember to watch, listen and learn –

life is much simpler that way."

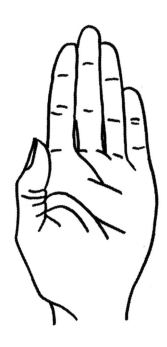

Chapter 7

The angel brushed the dirt off the wind blown robe

and looked up with a smile.

Then looking across the room,

the angel confidently walked to a small lacquer chess table.

Finely carved jade chessmen lay scattered on the chess board.

The angel picked up the pieces

and placed all of them in their proper places.

Then the angel picked up a dark pawn

and placed it two spaces ahead.

In deep thought the angel asked,

"Dear God, if I listen,

how do I make my dreams happen?"

The table began to shake.

The chessmen faltered and fell over.

The angel grabbed the edge of the table to be steadied.

For a minute the earth trembled and the heavens shook.

Then as abruptly as the quake began, it subsided.

The angel straightened up

and placed all the chess pieces back in their places.

The voice answered,

"The strength of the mind and the strength of the will

are the keys to manifesting.

For this, grounding—to be at peace—is absolutely necessary.

There is nothing more powerful than thought.

Think positive, happy thoughts always.

To manifest or create:

1. Think about what you would like and be specific.

2. Extend your senses to see it and feel it.

3. Do it with love.

4. And it appears.

Be swift in thought and be ready at any moment.

Within, lies all knowledge.

We have the power within ourselves.

Learn confidence, to rely on yourself and trust in yourself.

All things are an illusion and dreams do become reality.

Expand your consciousness

and be ready to accept anything at anytime.

Not by might but by the spirit of understanding,

God conquers the unthinkable.

He achieves the greatest, in ways unknown to man.

Believe and all things will come to pass.

All too often the ways are not established in our minds,

but in our hearts and this is what God follows.

Rest assured that God knows what we all want

even if we do not understand.

The Angel Asked God

It is therefore of great care and importance

that you do not judge people before your own eyes

but before the eyes of God.

Love thy fellowman always, wherever you go

and much greater achievements can be made.

Achievements far beyond the reaches of anyone's imagination

can be accomplished.

In reality the essence of what is and what we are, is;

faith, good mercy, love and understanding.

All of this makes us who we are and all things possible.

The self concept is merely in relation or terms

of what we think and know at the time.

Success depends on how much one believes in oneself

and not in what others think

Nobody but you can do that.

Continuously spiral upwards in thought.

The lessons to be learned are all necessary steps

for the progress of the human soul.

Lesson #1   You think as you are.

Lesson #2   You are able to change all things.

Anything is possible with God because God fears nothing.

Thoughts are realities, if we wish them.

Only those that realize this concept can understand

and will take upon that challenge to make their dreams come true.

God grants all wishes in true hearts.

Today is but a miracle,

yesterday is but a dream

and tomorrow envision the impossible!

Dreams do exist and come true in people's minds and hearts."

Chapter 8

The Angel Asked God

With a deep breath and shoulders back,

the angel walked across the room to the open window.

In a small planter under the sill,

were two tiny green leaves dividing the earth.

A small piece of dirt weighed down the delicate leaves.

The angel brushed the dirt of the budding vine

and then asked,

"Dear God, if my dreams can come true,

how long do I have to wait?"

A gentle breeze entered from outside.

It was warm and had the fresh scent of spring.

The early morning sun shone through the window,

striking the newly sprouted leaves.

Then the voice answered,

"Be patient. Time is an enemy or a friend.

It is your choice in the matter.

Patience is a virtue and a fortitude.

All things come to those who wait and listen.

Be patient and continue forward.

Follow your path and your dreams will follow and come true.

Focus your mind on day to day things

and don't let go of your dreams.

Be at peace with yourself and then others will follow.

Peace must prevail before true joy and happiness can follow.

Vera Littlewood

When one is in the understanding of peace and tranquility,

God is better known and understood.

All things in life are synchronized events

and it takes time to put them into place.

Some are not instant,

but for others they can miraculously occur in one moment of time.

All things have a time and place that must be followed.

The Angel Asked God

Delay does not necessarily mean a shortcoming

but may simply mean delay.

Keep faith.

Faith is only faith when there are no options.

The light always shines through darkness.

If we fear the dark,

then we only feed it more negativity.

Keep brief, positive affirmations always – they do help.

God will guide you.

You need only listen.

When one door closes, another door opens –

it has to—it is the law of nature.

Learn from your mistakes.

We are all learning

and by our mistakes we can make changes.

Something gained, something lost.

Something learned, something tossed.

The joys of life follow sorrow.

Time is a great healer.

Vera Littlewood

Above all else smile, it will help you.

Believe in yourself and all is well.

Rest in peace knowing this—

God's love will uphold you forever."

The Angel Asked God

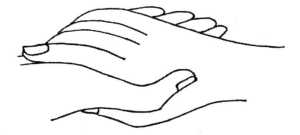

Chapter 9

The Angel Asked God

The angel stood pondering the tiny green growth,

basking in the sunlight.

Then the angel gazed through the window.

A beautiful clear blue sky surrounded the magnificent sun.

With shoulders straight and head held high,

the angel turned around and faced the mirror.

The sunlight glazed the mirror

and only a bright glare of sunshine reflected back.

The angel closed both eyes to protect against the brilliant light

and then asked,

"Dear God, you say that you love me,

but what do you mean by love?"

The Angel Asked God

Total silence filled the room.

The sun's glistening rays shone brilliantly before the mirror.

Then the sunlight moved and touched the angel's head and body.

A white luminescent light engulfed the angel.

The angel opened both eyes

and saw a rainbow of colors dancing in the light.

Slowly the light faded and a golden aura surrounded the angel.

Then the voice answered,

"God always loves us.

We are all his people.

God loves everyone and is with you.

God loves his people and provides for their needs.

He has a special journey for each one of us.

The Angel Asked God

It is about each one of us to create what our wishes are

and be granted through God.

He wishes the best for us.

Everything on earth has been created by God for good,

not evil intentions and so it should be lived accordingly.

God loves all creatures, great and small

and for those alike, kindness must always be given.

Vera Littlewood

Love yourself.

Keep peace and then love and understanding shall follow

beyond your wildest dreams imaginable.

Love is all around us,

if we only want it to be.

Love exists in more ways than one.

Love is the key

and laughter is the heart of every soul.

All things in life are based on love.

Love is far greater and exceeds all other powers of the universe.

Love emerges truth, and finds an answer.

Always beneath the surface is understanding.

Resolve issues in love.

Tolerance is a result of love balance.

In order to receive love, truth and honesty;

one must be able to give those things first.

Seek love and it seeks you.

Love is a hurtful and painful thing at times,

but once realized,

love is a far greater thing than we imagined it to be.

God's love is the only answer and love doesn't die.

Love is not to be understood in people's minds yet

until they can fathom all the riches in heaven and earth

and to the depths of hell frozen over.

The time traveler remembers only this:

Peace, tranquility and love—

the joyous love in our hearts."

Vera Littlewood

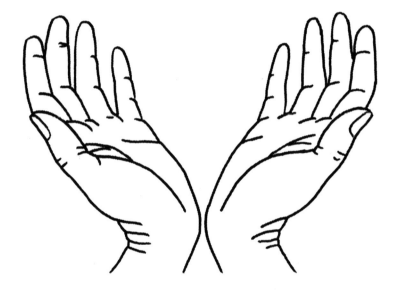

The angel smiled and then looked in the mirror.

Reflected back was a beautiful angelic form.

There were wings on that human being!

Vera Littlewood

The Angel Asked God

...and so in pondering our human destiny, I wrote these words,

Destiny

Together may we find,

the answers that we need.

Alone we also can,

but lonely, yes indeed.

V. Littlewood

About the Author

Vera Littlewood was raised in a Christian home. After studying Christianity, she became a confirmed Lutheran in her teenage years and applied her beliefs by teaching Sunday School.

In the following years she furthered her religious studies with meditational techniques. Taking an interest in the field of para-psychology, Vera studied the psychic fields under the instruction of several ministers.

An education in Microbiology science and general sciences became a useful resource in understanding metaphysical science techniques.

As a devout Christian, Vera has continued to study other religions, including Buddhism and Eastern philosophies.

A creative interest in the arts including writing, acting, modeling and drawing has lead to the completion of the book, The Angel Asked God.

Miracle upon miracle has been witnessed on a daily basis.

It is considered in the author's view, that God's hand can be seen everywhere and miracles surround us, just waiting to be seen.